Compass

Compass

FINDING THE WAY HOME
FROM THE INSIDE OUT

YASMIN GERMAINE HAUT

Epigraph Books
Rhinebeck, New York

Compass: Finding the Way Home From the Inside Out
Copyright © 2019 by Yasmin Germaine Haut

All rights reserved. No part of this book may be used or reproduced in any manner whatsoever without written permission except in the case of brief quotations em-bodied in critical articles or reviews.

This book is a work of fiction. Names, characters, businesses, organizations, places, events and incidents either are the product of the author's imagination or are used fictitiously. Any resemblance to actual persons, living or dead, events, or locales is entirely coincidental.

For information contact :
Yasminhaut@gmail.com
http://www.yasminhaut.com

Cover design by Emily Zebel
Cover art by Rahmana Marcia Graff
Book design by Colin Rolfe

ISBN: 978-1-948796-89-7
Library of Congress Control Number: 2019912016

First Edition: August 2019

Epigraph Books
22 East Market Street, Suite 304
Rhinebeck, New York 12572
(845) 876-4861
epigraphps.com

*For my Mother, Rose Jenny Preto Haut
who taught me about gardens.*

CONTENTS

Introduction ix

THE PIN AT THE CENTER 1
Appreciation for Gravity   5
Buzzing Gyroscope   8
Mascara   10
The Weight of Waiting   12
Dervish in a Blanket   14

THE PERIMETER 17
The Cat Bite   21
Seeds   24
Break a Code   26
Pollinators, Cousins and Internment   28
Elephant and Assassin   31
Prostration of a Sunflower   33
The Science of Meringue   35

STEPPING OUT 37
Butter   41
Bewildered Cassiopeia   43
No Guard Rails   46
Sheathed   48

BEYOND	51
The Eighth Sacrament	55
Face Paint	57
Soft Edges	59
Compass	61
Final Musings	65
Endnotes	67
About the Author	71
Acknowledgments	73

INTRODUCTION

We are ever turning. Seen and unseen, everywhere and everything, expressing itself in form and then spiraling out. Planets, seasons - all turning, transforming, changing.

We cannot register this turning. Scientists tell us that the human organism does not have the sensory equipment to identify movement unless relative to something stable.

Maybe that's a good thing. Standing at the equator, we are spinning at about 1000 miles an hour. And the earth is also hurtling around the sun at approximately 67,000 miles per hour, while the solar system spirals through the Milky Way.

And this is just astronomy. Politics, psychology, technology, spirituality - all are subject to this turning.

To be without movement is to decay. And even in decay, there is a turning, a composting, preparation for what is next. The planet is programmed to digest what is and what was; turning it over and over.

Living with great privilege, beauty, and security in my Central Pennsylvania home, I recognize how our culture is standing at an edge. I can no longer live as though our children will inherit the same world. Seeking a new way forward, I am asked to explore beyond my most precious ideas and ideals. I must recalibrate my navigational tools in order to move forward.

These poems, divided into four sections, are meant to explore this process of personal and impersonal recalibration, evolution, revolution.

I observe my identities and my sense of belonging shift and expand, reconnect, and reorient. The point of the compass quivers with each transition then recalibrates spiraling out with ever-expanding horizons.

After each poem, a reflection is offered. These are not about *doing*. There is too much *doing* in our lives. While reading, relax your hands, your feet, the muscles in your face. No need to do, or go, and no need to respond with the proper expression. Poetry is about being, feeling the gift of incarnation through all our senses, balancing in this fleeting moment of be-ing-ness.

Think of these reflections as an invitation to release what is no longer working. Can we fashion new ways to turn toward the future with fresh eyes and with an openness to all of your senses.

One

THE PIN AT THE CENTER

THE PIN AT THE CENTER

Bismillah[1] *Holy Quran*

Great imagination has fueled great progress. Such a dizzying enterprise this being human, turning through the cosmos on this spinning planet!

What keeps us from flying off into deep space with unbridled delight and wonder at our advances, the mystery, the possibilities?

In the past, we were girded by the daily pursuit of food, a mate, the preservation of our DNA. We remained pinned to our instincts. And they kept us relatively safe. However, as life evolved and the seasons turned, we transitioned from four-legged to two-legged, head over heart. Homo sapiens developed mastery over simple survival skills. As the brain enlarged, so did the heartaches.

Deep-seated instincts and insecurities linger. Securely myelinated, they live as neural pathways ever ready to pounce. But new assignments are added: relationship, community, love, harmony, and beauty, as conscious acts.

Looking up at the night sky, I feel the immensity of this human project. Similarly, when I hear a student's stunning question or gaze into a newborn's eyes, I slip into an expanded state of awe. I float above the details of today's tasks, astounded by some membrane that both contains and shelters.

Still, most days, I remain pinned to the minutiae of daily living grounding me, and if I am not careful, grinding me. I pay my taxes, brush my teeth, and pull weeds just like you. I am located; for the moment, pinned to the center.

Appreciation for the Gravity

Gravity holds us
like a mother's arms to this earthiness.
We measure, mine and calibrate
as though the weight
of in-formation might be a proxy
for the mass of her wisdom and prudence.

We cut and paste, mound and excavate.
We fabricate a world of time, place, form.

We manufacture arms.
Arms ticking and telling of time running out,
reaching for true north,
judging cardinal points,
suggesting,
orienting,
grasping,
pointing,
pinching,
prodding toward imaginary lines
on a map.

Yasmin Germaine Haut

> Still no matter how we cavort,
> Our Great Mother's Arms hold us close.
> She listens for the rhythms of heart,
> breath,
> seasons,
> moons.
> A deep listening for pulsing blood,
> until it's not.
> And even then,
> what was once in-formed
> she composts
> in the depths
> of her tumbling round landscape.

REFLECTION

Locating ourselves in space and time is our first test as our souls incarnate. The pin gets set in the center of our being, and we begin the tasks. Who am I? How do I navigate here and now?

Little by little, I arrive. I occupy the body and the conditions of my world. That is, until change scrambles the settings. Then, the inner compass must recalibrate. Physical, emotional, and cognitive habits must reset.

Buddhist teacher, Pema Chodron calls this a "gap".[2] Our lives get shook up. The "stranger" arrives and throws open the doors and windows. Impermanence makes itself known. We can accept the opportunity or add to our suffering by clutching and contracting. A momentary awareness arises. Old paradigms are questioned. Here we refresh, choose, regain personal authorship. We get to start over. We recalibrate.

I begin here because our very birth was just that; a reset button for our family, our neighborhood, our soul. Ah, the soul, held and set free, bound, incarnate, yet tethered to some mystery.

Consider.

Yasmin Germaine Haut

Buzzing Gyroscopes

Ready or not.
Center or not.
Circling some question
like a swarm seeking their Queen.

Empty of intelligence and
full of embodied longing.
My body, your body, nobody's,
and all bodies, planets, and stars.

Sometimes outside my self,
your self
and those others too.
We circle as a silent gravity engraves, loops, arcs,
epicenters, radiating and pulsing,
pulsars from a distant alien instinct,
aching, arching.

These buzzing gyroscopes
tethered to tissue from deep desire.
Lured by beauty,
gathering pollen,
offering honey.

REFLECTION

Jelaluddin Rumi suggests that we are ever searching for a way to return to a state of "Union." Pulled from the reed bed, orphaned, and living what appears to be a separate existence, we seek our way home.[3] We hunger for connections, roots, acceptance. Our parents, our family, neighborhood, and friends assist; sometimes with grace, sometimes with tribulations. The pin, carefully placed by our parents, keeps us tethered to them, their values, their world view. We explore as best we can.

So many lures distract and confuse. Eventually, like a butterfly meandering, we catch a scent. The expedition begins.

Can we begin to recognize distractions before we initiate a chase? Can we name the lessons learned in the journey? Can we embrace the feeling that we are in the midst of a great experiment - spirit incarnate, trying to remember "Union?"

Consider.

Yasmin Germaine Haut

Mascara

Beauty is a responsibility.
It follows you like a peacock's tail.
A hundred mascara-lashed eyes,
watching
with a hazy gaze.
An opiate
luring you from behind.
Trailing your every move.
Ensnaring with the ruse of conquest.
"Beware" she jeers.

Beauty entices.
It dangles
like fringe on a hijab.
Swaying.
Mesmerizing.
Bewildering.
I whisper
"Beneath that veil, we are all the same."
"We've all dug graves,
wrestled wars,
hungered at the banquet,
failed our hearts' desire,
quarreled with disease."

Gazing into her darkened eyes
a caravan of women to the horizon
turning over their shoulder
encouraging me on.
Beauty is salvation.

REFLECTION

The pull of beauty can be a salvation or a diversion. Negotiating her many guises, we come to see how this power can inspire or possess.

Beauty can take the form of a taste, small sounds or an orchestra. It can be a kind word, a sunset or a sweet smell. I often suggest that everyone create at least one beautiful thing a day. It can be as simple as a plate of food, or a kindness.

In all these forms beauty charms. Drawn by its mysteries, we feel a yearning to get close, to possess, to acquire, to replicate. And to accomplish this, we find ways to be suitable, at times abandoning essential parts of our unique nature. We aim to belong, to concede to a convention, to seize, and at times to merge. What is the cost?

Can we deepen our attention to the effects of beauty upon us? What are we willing to abandon in the presence of beauty? What is the gain?

Consider.

Yasmin Germaine Haut

Weight of Waiting

On an island
where they are force-feeding detainees,
Mothers and Fathers are counting the pages
in their ration book,
wondering if they'll have sufficient
beans and rice.

All this while I contemplate the privilege of
fasting this month of Ramadan.

I am bewildered with last night's dream
when an attitude of hunger and thirst
for justice sake,
shook my sensibilities.
What right do I have to fast?

On an island
where children are roaming the Malecon
kicking soccer balls,
and practicing with their ballet troupe,
walls crumble,
rooftops sag,
paint peels from giant ornate doors
as though scorched
by the heat
of a mighty hubris.
The weight of waiting for these feuds to end.

REFLECTION

The weight of waiting is so familiar, like a heavy backpack we no longer notice. We accommodate to its inconvenience and bear the burden.

I traveled to Cuba in 2011. There is no way to express the emotional weight of the island. Bearing the affliction of an old feud the island is heavy with dust, crumbling walls, peeling paint, hungry children; while the crystalline waters of the Caribbean comb the sandy beaches and crash her old stone walls.

Can we see where habits, conveniences, and comforts can build walls, prohibiting flow, compassion, harmony?

Where and to whom is an inquiry, an apology, a realignment calling? Or is there an inner voice walled off due to its painful nature? Does this inner voice have an important message?

Consider.

Yasmin Germaine Haut

Dervish in a Blanket

My daddy had just died.
My Mamma was sad.
I was staying with cousins.

Mamma came home,
a bundle in her arms.
I'd forgotten.
She laid him in my lap.

Some 56 years later
I still recall
a humid breeze,
sweet,
like breath,
in and out,
across the window ledge.

Holding my baby brother in my lap
I wondered.
Is this still a family?

No father.
A mother sad and solitary,
A big brother tearful and bewildered.
A new baby, fragile and sweet-smelling.

Compass

>   It's just a thin membrane,
>   crowded with comings and goings.
>   Looking into a baby's eyes you might think
>   birth is a miracle.
>
>   I got a hunch
>   on the other side
>   they're murmuring the same thing about death.
>   Scratching their heads,
>   wondering what happens
>   after you're born?

REFLECTION

Some say the dervish stands at the threshold between worlds. Austere, indifferent to dogma, theology, or intellect, the dervish is absorbed in the ways of the heart.

My baby brother invited me back into the world my father left. This bundle of baby repaired my inner compass. And his arrival focused me on the mysteries of the doorway between life and death.

Can you recall the first experience you had with a dying friend, relative, pet, idea? Are the qualities of the experience purged or cultivated in your current state? Is there work to be done here? Head above heart will not answer these mysteries. No words. No logic. This is the work of the heart.

Consider.

Two
THE
PERIMETER

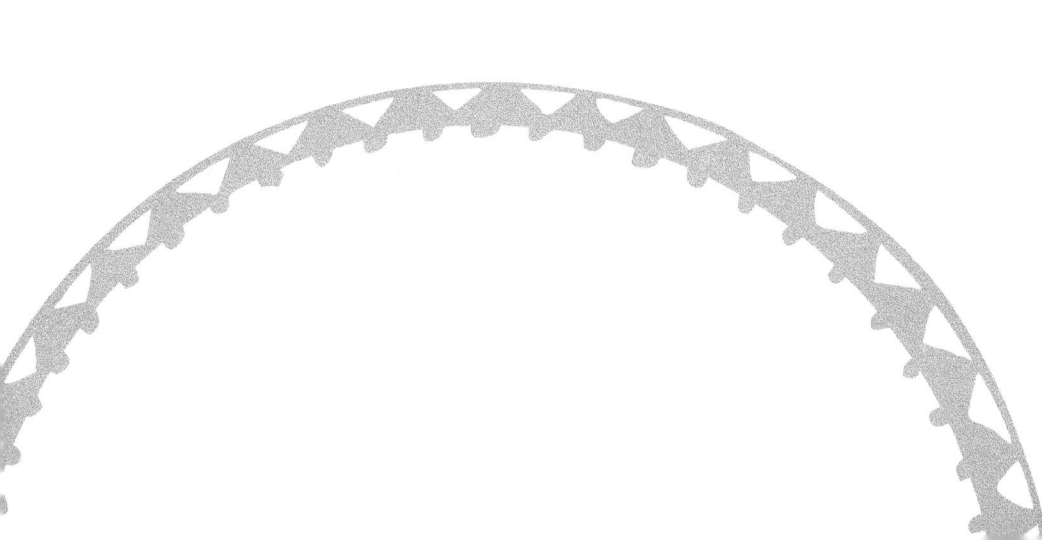

THE PERIMETER

Gate. Gate. Paragate. Parasamgate. Bodhi Svaha.[4] —Heart Sutra

Little by little, I learned that there were edges to my world. As soon as I was old enough, I approached, tentative, and curious. Everything appeared to have a beginning and an end, a definition, a perimeter, boundaries sharply delineated.

My neighborhood was familiar. I knew what belonged where and how to spiral out from my house to school, dance class, church, grandparents, and cousins. But I began to feel the pull of something more. There was some broader horizon upon which the foreground of life was staged.

To this daughter of the '60s, boundaries were an enticement, an invitation. Approaching an edge meant excitement, maybe danger. But approaching the edge also insinuated some magnificence, scenarios unavailable on the inside.

Yasmin Germaine Haut

I spiraled outward slowly, sniffing the air, checking for the smell of other hearths, watching for footprints, listening for birds and insects.

I checked my compass. And with the help of mentors, friends, and intuition, I discovered ways to remain tethered while noticing the essential characteristics of an edge.

The Cat Bite

A domesticated animal is still an animal.
A fire is still a fire.
Even when contained in our furnace
or beneath the tea kettle, it remains hot.

My cat bit me this week.
There was no other way to say "enough."
As the superior one, rational and parental, I pushed.
Just one more claw.

Do I love him more, less?
(Do these questions apply to love?)

His ancestral roots flourish,
claws and teeth
wired for the tasks of food.
Despite the bowl of kibble,
he is still like the fire in the woodstove,
contained
but full of heat and spark.

Sleeping at my feet each morning,
purrs and cuddles,
cold nudging nose
soft coat.
Ah, this is why we allow you here.

Yasmin Germaine Haut

(Is the myth of domestication a joke we play on ourselves?
Wanting to coax the wildness out
we invent dependency and coddle.)

No, I love him more today.
This bite I am tending
adds dignity to my feelings for him.

Now, you and me,
from many different castes and clans,
histories of scarcity and peril,
harvests and celebrations,
seed gatherers,
wind watchers,
scanning the news,
sniffing the air.

What lays purring on my bedcovers
Wanting the nod of dignity?

What wild darling has had enough grooming?

REFLECTION

In our earthly form, we all have edges; where we begin and end, and where our tolerance begins and ends. Just by living our lives, we seem to rub up against each other's boundaries.

The edges become more apparent with technology. Greater proximity, even if it's virtual proximity, brings increased awareness. Bouts of judgment, aspersions, and the habit of comparing and contrasting can lead us toward tolerance or set battle lines. The immense range of cultures, religions, dress, gender identifications, etc, can either lock us in our tribal towers or expand us by polishing our heart.

Do you know your edges? What are your triggers? Do you stand on a moral "high ground" that divides you from others? Can you begin to recognize habituated behaviors that lead to suffering? Can you allow neighbors, loved ones, those who challenge, to have their edges? Can you feel the edge and maintain a calm breath?

Consider.

Yasmin Germaine Haut

Seeds

I dreamt last night of seeds,
little ones with fairy wings,
shiny sea beans,
floating between continents.

I dreamt of dark earth,
thick roots in ancient braids,
holding back the stream bank,
filament-like roots,
fine as strands of light.

I reached into the soil of my dream.
I filled my hands with a harvest of gemstones
pushed to the surface from the winter's freeze.
I tossed them upward.
I watched them turning like sky around the North Star.
Or was it a secret turning in me?

REFLECTION

While preparing the garden for spring, I am struck by the many rocks and stones that appear. They were not in the soil last fall. They are birthed from last winter's freeze.

I pull the tools from the shed and begin.

What gets removed, what gets harrowed? Are there treasures to be harvested?

I turn the soil and yesterday's compost shines, rich and willing.

And in your inner garden, what has the seasons' turn brought to the surface? Will you cultivate, harrow, purge, treasure?

Consider.

Yasmin Germaine Haut

Break a Code

Climbing stairs
I find my mind was trained
to know a certain spacing
and it is not here.
Out of rhythm, I trip and fumble.

Focus on that step,
then this one.
But the cadence I have come to depend on
is gone.
I falter.

Likewise
the time of day confounds me.
I am left with only the slant of light,
hunger, and sleep to navigate the day's rhythm.

The sounds of palm fronds like white noise
to my monkey mind,
drowning in tidal pools.

Blue everywhere,
and purple
or is that green, no grey.
Dizzying mandalas!
I give up.
Unable to name and conquer the colors with words.

Compass

Colored pencils,
Mayan fabric,
flashes of dreams,
these will have to suffice.

Drunk with it all.
New senses arise
like smoke on a distant horizon,
suggesting a primitive hearth
where someone or thing
is struggling to nourish a family.
Nerve endings open
like underground rivers
waiting for a code to be broken.

REFLECTION

From the moment of birth, our neurology is busy making sense of the myriad of sensations coming at us. We label, codify, and attempt to control all the spoken and unspoken agreements.

My first trip to the Yucatan was an adventure in letting go of a world that was limited but comfortable. Shaking up my sensibilities, I relaxed into the beauty around me and learned to break a new code embedded in the beauty and harmony of the landscape and language.

Neural pathways previously hardwired didn't work. They fire with ease and confidence, but - they kept me locked in a world that was limiting and inflexible.

What codes rule our lives? Are these serving or sheltering us?

Consider.

Yasmin Germaine Haut

Pollinators, Cousins, and Internments

As long as I remember, there was a garden.
Our garden was the background
to the little pool we inflated
when the days were steamy.

The garden's sheer vitality
fed the passion that grew in us
for a world of green,
rich dirt,
and buzzing pollinators.

The annual turning of earth, buds, and blossoms
marked the years,
and still do.
Smells, color, and shape
remind me of moods,
and have become my mantra.

Memories blossom in an April garden.
The blush of lilac comes and goes,
fading into heart-shaped leaves.
Azalea donates a flourish of color.
Hostas open out, plump and full of themselves.
Lilies of the valley lurk in the shadowy places,
with memories of other outings
to the family gravesites.

Compass

Back then
aunts and cousins gathered buckets of flowers
after Sunday Mass.
A great adventure for my cousins, and for me.

We romped through a meadow of sad aunts and uncles.
Gay and light,
feeling air and sun and scent,
radiating from each other.

These folks we hardly knew
Interned beneath the markers and flowers.
A mystery we barely paused to consider.

Today rose plants and fig tree cuttings,
hosta, azaleas, lilies of the valley and lilacs
carefully transplanted from Mom's garden
all waking up in the soil
I cultivate.

Mom's garden is being laid to rest.
Her house will be sold.
There are no hands to pull the weeds
No one to stake tomatoes.

My garden will feed the buckets for gravesite trips.
So, it is left to us to welcome the pollinators.

Yasmin Germaine Haut

REFLECTION

As a child, I grew up visiting the family gravesite as part of our Sunday morning ritual in summer. We pranced around the graveyard. We became familiar with death, a boundary we decorated with forsythia, old fashioned roses, and daisies.

Standing at my parent's' graves, I feel the pull of their DNA in my triumphs and my failings. I feel the rumbling in my belly; considering my imperfections as a daughter, niece, grandchild, sister. The jumble of esteem, impudence, vigilance, absence, and tenderness softens in a pool of warmth and gratitude.

Are your ancestor's alive in you? In what ways do you experience this? Or not? Would some ritual of remembrance for your ancestors enhance anything you wish to cultivate in your garden?

Consider.

Elephant and Assassin

Rich and black and velvety,
    the Elephant Ear waves in the October warmth,
    unaware
    of looming danger.

Nearly everything else has been cleared away.
Only the chaos of tangled weary stalks,
    rotting fruits,
    seasoned with random seeds
    remains.
A lone Elephant Ear
like a sentinel
    standing dazed,
    listening
    for the final trumpet.

Some strange courage
maintains this perfect posture.

While the first freeze lurks
like an assassin's bullet,
    poised to shoot,
    draining
    all vigor
    from the listening ears.

Yasmin Germaine Haut

REFLECTION

To fully possess this gift of life is also to appreciate how each day we die a little bit.

Realizing the temporary nature of our physical existence is humbling and motivating. The great circle is ever-present, yet easily ignored, until the assassin strikes.

Until then, we gather in the clear, precious vision of the present moment. We gaze at nature standing tall, equanimous, dazzling, elegant. Free from anxiety and full of a mighty vigor, nature inspires.

Old scripts rattle through the mind, whispering of danger, demise, loss. Simultaneously visions of grandeur bolster our resolve: a smiling pansy, blue speckled eggs in the nest, the smell of summer rain, crystalline designs on a winter windowpane, crisp fallen oak leaves. Inayat Khan suggests that the Book of Nature is the only scared text.[5]

How do I animate my aliveness while recognizing it is a temporary condition? Can I turn through the seasons of life vulnerable and open to each unique moment? Can I learn from the audacity of Nature's resilience, power, flexibility?

Consider.

Prostration of a Sunflower

She opened proud and determined
facing the sun.
Greeting goldfinch, bees, worms, ants
and humans
with equal bearing.
She stands for beauty.

Then the storm came.
And she yielded,
prostrating herself in the garden.

We humans are neophytes at surrender.
While she cannot avoid the storm,
we run for cover.

The soil washes away at her feet.
Gallantly she stands in the foaming tides.
Birth and death
until she can no longer.
Bending, heavy head to the mud.

The sun returns.
I lift the blossom's face to the sky.
I tie her to the fence post.
And her mood brightens
and bees hum: Hu![6]

Yasmin Germaine Haut

REFLECTION

Which of my roles in the world define me? Do these roles shield me from other ways of knowing myself? The characters I play, my surroundings, and cultural conventions are essential, but can be limiting.

The future requires that we cultivate a pearl of deeper wisdom. Wisdom which evolves from the inside out. This wisdom is rooted in self-awareness. It requires a willingness to explore the crevices, caves, and caverns where yearnings, fears, intimacies, and interdependence mingle.

Can I prostrate myself, head below heart, and surrender to some inner antagonist yet to be discovered?

Yes, courage and a dose of adventure, fearlessness, and perhaps madness are required.

Consider.

The Science of Meringue

If you resign to the snow
does spring get stuck in last year's crusty seed pods?
If you deny the rain
do the storm clouds forget how wetness longs for the sea?
When tomorrow's sun rises,
and my heavy head still lays on the pillow,
will stars sprinkle from the showerhead
when my lover takes her morning shower?

My stories can't halt the season's turn
or the ocean's churn.
My lover washes her hair
with the usual spray of warm water and suds
despite my morning musings.

Stories are the melodious score I hum
when the day gets tedious.
A score will never even the odds;
but oddly
even out the tendency to feel scorn
for shortcomings and imperfections.
Still, to hum or whistle will often turn a smile.

Yasmin Germaine Haut

> No matter what story I tell,
> one day folds into another.
> Fluffy, temperamental egg whites
> forget their airy nature as they meld with sticky syrup.
> Just a few moments in the oven
> and the meringue is set.

REFLECTION

Stories are an age-old scheme we use to explore and make friends with experience and mystery. Every story is like a magic spell arranging and relating, weaving, and reminding us of what we want remembered, learned, engraved.

Each time we retell a story, we emblazon the characteristics of the story in our psyche, shaping history into our particular version of the truth.

I suspect the truth is a landscape more vast than any single story we tell. Ideas and ideals imbedded in our small stories can limit and mislead. What remains outside the story can never be known unless we pause to reconsider.

Can you explore a story you tell about yourself or the people around you? Are there ways the story concretizes a belief that is no longer true? Or does the story constrain your perceptions of the way forward?

Consider.

Three

STEPPING OUT

STEPPING OUT

*Out beyond beyond ideas of wrongdoing and right-doing,
there is a field. I will meet you there.*[7] —Rumi

As soon as I was old enough, I gathered courage where I could find it. I approached the boundary waters of the world and noticed the shoreline, the waves, and the mysterious depths. Hesitant and curious, I began a new expedition and stepped out.

I learned that the definitions, dogmas, ideas, and ideals, which had served me all these years, were perched on soft and wet earth. There was a livingness which hinted at something more. An ever-widening landscape slowly appeared. I'm confident that pictures from the Apollo Mission and latter from the Hubble Telescope were vital in this evolution. To this day, seeing those startling photos stirs some deep longing. I am propelled beyond my small ego attachments.

At first awkward and at times hurtful to the people who wished to protect me from the unknown, I left the familiar. They argued and attempted to persuade me of the ultimate truth of their rules and methods. I ventured out.

To this day, I am saddened by the trail of tears this leaving caused the people I love. Behind me and hidden inside me, like a river flowing, winding through and around obstacles, and eventually back to the vast sea, these waters rose.

Butter

In the late summer window
A quarter-pound of butter wants to keep
its square corners,
a habit from Military School.
But the recipe says:
"carefully fold the butter into the light,
cool the air with your equanimity."

Julien's tiny toes
like telescopes are searching.

Halter that stead.
Clean the litter.
Bring in the sheep.
The sky is changing.

Yesterday's moon
has lost a dollop of light.
It is stuck in the astronomer's eye.
She tries to pour her long night dream
back into the sky.

Julien's toes touch the ground.

Yasmin Germaine Haut

REFLECTION

Watch a baby's toes delicately searching, barely able to touch the ground. But, when they do, they seek sweetness, kindness, and adventure.

 The balance between safety and freedom is a challenge for all parents or anyone who is nurturing someone or something they love. Vulnerable and naïve, we spread our wings. And our loved ones watch with delight, with fear, and with apprehension.

 Julien is 10 years old now. But I can feel the lightness of his presence all those years ago. His little toes poked out the bottom of the blanket as we gazed at this miraculous arrival.

 And today I realize there is an inner community, a family of voices whispering, worrying, caring, delighting and conspiring with me.[8] This community is comprised of a child, physician, doctor, parent, judge and sometimes more. How am I balancing their need for sweetness, kindness, adventure, love?

 What nurtures your inner community's appetite for sweetness? How do you nurture your deepest desires? Does your yearning heart take you outside your comfort zone?

 Consider

Bewildered Cassiopeia

When a mother dies
the North Star disappears.
I find up, down, over and again scramble,
and I am amazed that gravity still holds.
I place one foot, then the other on the cool floor
beside my bed.
And an inner habit
points me in the direction of today's work.

Did I say work?
No.
What I mean is,
the sounds outside my window
are pulsing and promising.
There is no thing
and every thing
hidden
in this promise.

When a mother dies
the laws of physics reinvent themselves.
In her honor
the principle that draws matter into form
bends and crawls on its knees.

Yasmin Germaine Haut

No straight lines.
Only that which curves
and sways
makes its way into this dwelling space.
No angles, no corners.

When a mother dies
the astronomer bows to the astrologer,
who gets giddy with her newfound prestige.
She commands the constellations,
"Bow to your partner."
Pisces and Cassiopeia move
bewildered
across the sky.
"Turn to your corner," she sings.
Aries and Andromeda do-si-do.

They all spin and turn,
sway and pulse bewildered and ecstatic.
Dancing to the sounds outside my window,
circling some mysterious dark space,
deep space,
empty and full.

When a mother dies
so do daughters and sons.
We step over the edge.
A caravan of orphans now,
following whatever inspires
up ahead.

Compass

With time
the gaze turns upward.
New stars gathering fuel.
Some catch fire in our hearts,
and the heavens shift to recalibrate,
turning around a center.
Toward the One.

REFLECTION

Life happens. Parents die, children move out, illness strikes, jobs are lost, trees fall, crops fail. And in each one of these, we experience release. It happens over and over again.

For a moment weightless and giddy, nothing constricting, only a spiraling. Once firmly tethered by worldly definitions (family roles, class, education, etc.) I am liberated. The pin which helped me navigate now is released. The needle swings wildly.

Again, another pause. Like opening your eyes after a vast dream. Am I awake, or am I still dreaming? Some may say, "Die before you die." Or others may call this a version of the Bardo.[9] Whatever we name this state, it is a great moment to soften and allow the question to sink in. With courage, we release our habitual grasping and embrace uncertainty.

Consider.

Yasmin Germaine Haut

No Guard Rails

In the woods,
next to a rocky gorge,
rushing water below.

It's cool and green,
moist with no shafts of light
piercing the canopy,
just trees.
Many trees
interrupted by grey rock outcroppings,
some moss and not much other ground cover.

Consider going down?

"There are no guard rails,"
the woods whisper,
and this mantra imprints in my flesh.

I am a tree,
whose bark has been engraved.

Roots reaching,
grabbing, sipping and slipping;
On the edge.

REFLECTION

This is risky business. Exploring untethered does not discriminate outward and inward, up and down, good and bad, north and south.

We must develop increased awareness, and release duality as an organizing principle of the mind. Inventiveness, resiliency, patience, creativity is called to the front of the line. Our desire to know the answers compete with a willingness to live the question. Will there be a winner. Or is that paradigm also falling away?

Slippery? Yes. Like Julien's little toes, explore with caution, seek sweetness, kindness, adventure, love?

No guard rails here.

Much of our lives we gather information from the outside. What we gain in this process are facts, ideas, tidbits from others. Deep-knowing is embedded in the body. It requires careful listening, paying attention to all that arises - instinct, dreams, all the senses. Let's call this wisdom.

Here we harvest joys, and regrets, short-comings, and accomplishments. They may not define me, but I embrace what arises, and I mine them for clues.

Can you feel your roots going deep, not just beneath but also within.

Consider.

Yasmin Germaine Haut

Sheathed

There is an intimacy to the body
that remains so close,
its nature
must endure
undeciphered.

Linear ways of knowing
are foreign
to this familiarity,
like a code nesting
in the pulse of my veins,
yet as mysterious
as a distant black hole.
Or is it the opposite of a black hole,
all reflected light and no mass?
All wave, no particle?

One hand on my spleen and one on my heart,
I feel the rise and fall of breath,
enfleshed by this time and space phenomenon.
The noumenon sheathed,
like a blade whose wisdom
is too sharp to wield,
but perfect for nudging me.
Tapping toward coordinates on the map home.

REFLECTION

Does the absence of strict cultural rules, parental constraints, and religious dogma make us more vulnerable? Can we unsheathe the blade of truth and negotiate the world's edicts and orders with responsibility, kindness, humility?

Perhaps we learn to handle this blade, to live with vulnerability and courage. Perhaps we cease editing our heart's desire at the expense of belonging to familiarity, habits, and security.

Brene Brown calls this braving the wild.[10] In this way we recognize that real belonging starts with belonging to ourselves. We cease changing who we are and deepen our capacity to be who we are. Brown coins the wonderful phrase "soft front, strong back, wild heart."

Yes, many on the planet struggle to feed their families. They cannot protect their children from drones, cartels, gangs. The scourge of poverty, discrimination, and racism persists. My challenge is to remain centered and calm. All action must be rooted in wisdom, courage, and stability. This is the final chapter. I seek wise action, released from reactivity.

Can you recognize patterns motivated by fear and reactivity? Can you cultivate the courage necessary to wield the blade of truth; stand firm, patient, strong, yet soft, vulnerable, and valiant?

Consider.

Four
BEYOND

Compass

BEYOND

We saw to the edge of all there is — so brutal and alive it seemed to comprehend us back.[11] —Tracey K. Smith

Once outside the influence of an objects gravitational pull, we soar. This is true of physical objects as well as ideas, emotions, wounds, ideals, and even personal stories.

Nothing here to pawn the ego. No need to respond. No need to be right. The compass needle is untethered.

A personal retreat can have a similar effect. Alone in the retreat hut, only the arc of the sun to mark the passing days, a turning sky of stars and planets to chart the night, immeasurable distances, time. Our small stories soften into the incalculable. Everything appears alive and full of possibilities yet to be imagined.

Contemplating how often I have defended myself with ideas and clever arguments, I see how these conversations build walls. My ego tangles with itself. Rumi suggests that we sell this cleverness and buy bewilderment. Because once we have gathered the courage to explore beyond our comfort zone, awe and bewilderment are the only options, along with a big gulp of humility.

The pin in the center of the compass which was secured out of great love from our parents, family and friends' desire to keep us safe, must now retrofit! Listen to Greg Boyle, from Homeboy Industries..

> *"Humility returns the center of gravity to the center. It addresses the ego clinging, which supplies oxygen to our suffering. It calls for a light grasp. For the opposite of clinging is not letting go but cherishing. This is the goal of the practice of humility. That having a "light grasp" on life prepares the way for cherishing what is right in front of us.*[12]

Learning to cherish is the final assignment. No need to cling to the past. No need to hold any hostages. We are freed from impressions, judgments and dichotomies of right and wrong. Our circling brings us back to ourselves, humbled and awestruck. This is the exit ramp from despair. We learn humility. We recognize our interdependence. And we feel great gratitude for our ancestors who brought us this far.

Can I cherish my tribe, my wife, my beloved son, can I adore my kitties, my garden, the seasons, our blue oceans, and deep night sky without grasping? Can I carve a jewel out of my devotion to the planet, my relations, both known and yet unknown? Can I rest the pointer for my compass here, and follow this guidance where it leads?

The Eighth Sacrament

Clear the desk.
Break all the pencil points,
but save the erasers
and whatever bits of colored chalk
smudged on your fingertips.
The curriculum has grown stale.
We are tossing it out to the birds.

Next September you'll need only a small shovel,
a fingernail brush,
and some pots and pans.

When they calculate our success this time next year
they will measure
the height of the spinach,
the blush on our cheeks.
We will celebrate graduation
with the Eighth Sacrament –
A ritual to celebrate the first meal from our Spring Garden.

You will consider
the mysteries of those brown seeds,
warm earth,
sun and rain,
as you take your first bite.

Yasmin Germaine Haut

I will weep in the name of the Father,
the Mother,
and the Holiest of Children

REFLECTION

We have imagined schools largely as a system for instilling cultural values, facts we have gathered about how the world works, and how to manage and manipulate it. Yes, thankfully there are the liberal arts. And for this, we can be grateful as it opens us to music, literature, color and form, dance, etc.

But recent educational goals focus on math, science. and technology. In the Eighth Sacrament I suggest that we open education further to mystery. Wouldn't it be wonderful if we introduced gardening to the curriculum? The wonder of seeds sprouting and becoming food might develop awe and wonder. And we could measure our success by the literal fruits of our labor, cherishing each taste, color, smell.

The first harvest would be a sacramental moment, another pause.

Maybe you plant a garden. Or perhaps your neighbor shares some of their first tomatoes. Can you pause with that first bite, juicy and delicious, to appreciate this mysterious gift bestowed in gratitude for your participation in the continuous activity of creation?

Consider.

Face Paint

Eager tendrils ripening with fruit.
Feeding on yesterday's "normal."

Roots woven thick,
wanting to unveil
a new story of reaching without grasping,
of nutrients brewed
before such lying leaked.

Like shining from shook spoil,[13]
This new fruit has little taste.
Don't dip it in sacred honey pots.
I hear a stampede.
Throw the pots at their feet.
Let the insects feast and the dust swirl.
Create a paste of sweet earth and paint your faces, hands, and feet.

Then we can run out into the desert
followed by swarms of bees,
We can sing in a register
our ears are only beginning to hear.
Disguised and uninhibited
circling, humming, and sounding bells.

Yasmin Germaine Haut

REFLECTION

Discovering that our planet is round or that the earth revolves around the sun were significant psychological and spiritual shifts. Aftershocks crumbled many cultural and religious beliefs.

Similarly, the printing press, the Industrial Revolution, penicillin, electricity; all changed the world in ways that could not have been anticipated.

Science marches onward making some of life easier but raising more and more questions about our place in creation. Robotics will soon master many more tasks: jobs, housekeeping, driving, health care. Another great revolution is unfolding. What is essential? Where do I set true north? Or is this too a myth that has outlived its usefulness?

Consider.

Soft Edges

In the morning when I open my eyes
the edges of the room are soft and mysterious
as if a spreading fog is sent
to dispel the story of separation
between
table,
lamp,
sky,
earth,
you and me.

Today I touched a warm circle of soil with my fingers
to poke a hole for these tiny seeds,
remembering promises kept,
those broken and others we are yet to recall.

Our senses expanding and receding.
Tides, tracing patterns in the sand.

Stand at the center of these patterns.
Wield a shield of stardust
and a blue crayon for a sword.
Banish what is not braided from sea breeze,
from sunsets and from song.
And dance like dogs set loose at the beach for the first time.

Yasmin Germaine Haut

REFLECTION

When waking from a dream the world is less distinct and more sensuous. The brain is still floating in a sea of melatonin and the edges that separate are less distinct. Words become less precise and more transient.

Our language systems in the West developed exactitude and the capacity to engineer a world of science, mechanization, technology, and robotics. A question was to be solved, not contemplated.

Leonard Shlain[14] suggests that as we became more reliant on the specificity of words, especially the written word, our brains were pruned. Reliance on the senses changed, and the facility to observe and explore shifted to more of a mechanistic model.

In regions of the world where pictographs persist the right brain's capacity for intuition, reading animal behavior, predicting weather, decoding scents - all remain largely active. The alphabet had the opposite affect on brain development, parsing experience and information into chunks to be analyzed, utilized and eventually made into commodities. We drifted away from embodied wisdom.

What if we reclaimed these embodied aptitudes? What if we lived in awe of the questions? What if we cherished the not knowing and remained calm and curious?

Consider.

Compass

A rose face.
Perfectly formed,
round and elegant.
Heavy and cool in my hand
Solid
Poised.

Your graceful arm sweeps and steadies.
I am inspired.

My arms reach, toes point,
gaze stills,
breath like a metronome,
senses awaken,
sharpen.
Each tethered to an inner longing.

The adhan calls[15]
and a deep pining responds.
I recalibrate.
I am a compass.

Yasmin Germaine Haut

You may think of me as a dancer, a gardener, a yogi, mother, wife,
child...
And I am.
Heart cleaved, carved, scoured,
bathed in mother's milk,
polished by fine powder from distant star clusters.

My needle floats
on a heart space
serene and fragrant.
A lotus open to blue sky.

The pin in my center
knows the mysteries of the edge,
the dangers of false dogma,
the heartbreak of love,
the well stream of hope.

I point my whole self toward a new prayer.

REFLECTION

The compass needle is a small strip of metal, magnetized and floating frictionless on a small polished gem, a pivot point. The magnetic end of the needle points south. It is repelled by the magnetic force of the earth. The other end, usually painted red, points toward magnetic north.

We know compasses have aided explorers traversing deserts, oceans, mountain ranges, and undersea caverns. Nearly every place on earth has been explored using a compass due to the ubiquitous nature of the planet's magnetic field.

Can we learn to magnetize our inner wisdom? Can we polish our hearts so this wisdom floats frictionless in this milky pool of deep knowingness? Can we call upon the wisdom of nature to synchronize our inner compass?

Consider

FINAL MUSINGS

Our lives are the perfect curriculum for the lessons our souls seek. Old navigational tools have been a great boon. But lately we seem to be sailing in circles. Once steady and reliable, the needle pointed true north. The compass promised a way forward with relative security if I agreed to the rules. Ah, the rules!

I tell students to consider breaking one rule a day. All great discoveries require this willingness to recognize the impermanence of even our most revered ideas and ideals, rules and principles. Copernicus, Einstein, Darwin all made astounding discoveries that flew in the face of academic, ecclesiastic, and cultural norms. And it's likely that even these discoveries will be found incomplete.

We become the personal authors of our lives, our choices, our dreams. We step over the boundaries that once ruled our conscience and cultivate conscientiousness.

The pin at the center finds a way to pierce through the thick skin of old wounds, scar tissue, the residuals of histories, the pain of separations and losses. The compass rose is now bejeweled with gratitude, forgiveness, relationships, humility, interdependence.

Let's picture these qualities at the center of our individual compasses. Let's grow trust and make compassion the magnetic force that attracts the arm of our compass.

END NOTES

[1] Bismillah begins every sura of the Quran. You could translate this sacred phrase as, We begin in the name of Unity. For more of this discussion see Douglas-Klotz, Neil, Desert Wisdom: Sacred Middle Eastern Writings from the Goddess through the Sufis (San Francisco: Harper Collins, 1995).

[2] Pema Chodron discusses the importance of a *gap* in the linear progression of our lives. A gap occurs when we get turned around by some event. It may be a death, a loss of job or relationship, a sudden diagnosis. The foundations upon which our lives have been built are all effected by this gap. We reassess, realign, press the reset button.

[3] Jelaluddin Rumi is one of the best-selling poets of our time. He was a Sufi master in 12th century Afghanistan. His poems explore the desire to seek Unity with the Holy One and *describe the pain of living our lives as though separate.*

⁴ Gate, Gate, Paragate, Parasamgate, Bohdi Svaha is the final phrase of the Prajnaparamita (Heart Sutra). This is a beloved Buddhist prayer. One way of understanding these sounds is to go beyond, and even further beyond. Keep up the effort until we reach the shores of enlightenment.

The sutra suggests that releasing attachments and noticing our grasping nature is a vital practice. Impermanence is a fact of existence.

⁵ Hazrat Inayat Khan brought the Message of Unity to the west in the 1920s. He suggests that there is one Holy Book, unsurpassed. It is the Holy Book of Nature.

⁶ Hu is the mystical sound the Sufis use to praise the Holy One.

⁷ This is another beloved poem of Rumi which hints at the call to abandon polarities and meet with open hearts and minds.

⁸ Transpersonal as well as Sufi Psychology suggests that we must make deep inner peace before endeavoring to take on the task of world peace. Inviting all the inner voices to the table we create an internal group therapy session. I've found this work to be critical before stepping out into the wider world.

⁹ The Bardo is the experience after death and prior to rebirth. in Buddhist cosmology.

¹⁰ Brown, Brene, Braving the Wild: The Quest for True Belonging and the Courage to Stand Alone (New York: Random House, 2017).

¹¹ Smith, Tracey, Life on Mars (Minnesota, First Graywolf Printing, 2011).

[12] Boyle, Gregory, Barking at the Choir: The Power of Radical Kinship (New York: Simon and Schuster, 2017).

[13] Gerard Manley Hopkins describes the radical transformation of the world through the Industrial Revolution. He compares nuts, bolts and mechanics with the glory of God. In his poem God's Grandeur he uses the term, "like shining from shook foil" to characterize this massive transition. I have adjusted this phrase to point metaphorically toward our current ecological transition. Perhaps a culture built on false or half truths results in unripe or overripe produce. Hopkins, Gerard Manley. Poems. (London: Humphrey Milford, 1918).

[14] Shlain, Leonard, The Alphabet versus the Goddess: The Conflict Between Word and Image (New York: Penguin Group, 1998).

[15] Adhan is the Islamic call to prayer sung by the muezzin five times a day. While travelling in the Middle East I experienced this haunting sound as penetrating and enchanting.

ABOUT THE AUTHOR

Yasmin Germaine lives in Central Pennsylvania with her wife and two cats. She is a mother, a clinical social worker, gardener, yoga teacher and Sheikah with Sufi Ruhaniat International.

    This offering is an opportunity for her to share her poetry along with some of the themes she teachers and believes may be useful as we make our way toward greater understanding, compassion and generosity as a species. You can reach Yasmin Germaine at yasminhaut@gmail.com or www.yasminhaut.com.

ACKNOWLEDGMENTS

Many thanks to all my teachers, seen and unseen. Special gratitude to my wife, Kellie Majid Ananda Tikkun, my son Noah Stephen Whelan and, my initiator, Saadi Neil Douglas-Klotz. Also to Cara Meglio who offered her editing skills. I am grateful for Rahmana Marcia Rowe who complemented this work with her compass artwork and to Emily Zebel for her graphic design.

Finally, deep appreciation to the garden that feeds us, the animals that humor us, the trees that shelter us, and the skies that give us perspective.

www.ingramcontent.com/pod-product-compliance
Lightning Source LLC
Chambersburg PA
CBHW020950090426
42736CB00010B/1353